WELCOME, PROFESSIONAL PC... ...

THIS BOOK WILL BE YOUR LOYAL COMPANION DURING YOUR BATHROOM BREAKS.

IT WILL MAKE SURE THAT THE TIME SPENT ON THE TOILET BECOMES QUALITY TIME AND TIME FOR GROWTH.

IT WILL ALSO KEEP YOU AWAY FROM YOUR PHONE'S SCREEN, WHICH YOUR LOVELY FACE STARES AT FAR TOO OFTEN.

SO, SIT COMFORTABLY, TAKE A DEEP BREATH, CHALLENGE YOURSELF WITH THESE RIDDLES AND PUZZLES...

AND PUSH HARD IF NECESSARY!

THE BOOK IS DIVIDED INTO SEVERAL SECTIONS, EACH
WITH DIFFERENT CHARACTERISTICS. THE GOAL IS TO
NEVER LET YOU GET BORED AND TO GIVE YOU AS
MUCH STIMULATION AS POSSIBLE...

TO HELP YOU POOP.

RIDDLES

- LOGICAL
- PLAYFUL
- MATHEMATICAL
- GENERAL CULTURE

PUZZLES

- LOGICALLY DEDUCTIVE
- LINGUISTIC
- GEOMETRIC
- PHILOSOPHICAL
- PRACTICAL
- SEQUENCES
- COMBINATORIAL LOGIC

PARADOXES AND CURIOSITIES

LOGICAL
RIDDLES

WELCOME TO THE LOGICAL RIDDLES SECTION, WHERE EACH PUZZLE STIMULATES YOUR THINKING AND TESTS YOUR REASONING SKILLS. HERE YOU'LL FIND CHALLENGES THAT REQUIRE ATTENTION TO DETAIL, DEDUCTION, AND A BIT OF CREATIVITY TO REACH THE SOLUTION. GET READY TO SOLVE INTRIGUING AND FUN PROBLEMS THAT WILL MAKE YOU THINK AND, AT THE SAME TIME, POOPING

1
IF AN ELECTRIC TRAIN IS TRAVELING SOUTH, IN WHICH DIRECTION DOES THE SMOKE GO?

_____

2
WHAT BELONGS TO YOU BUT IS MOSTLY USED BY OTHERS?

_____

3
IF THERE ARE 5 APPLES IN A BASKET AND YOU TAKE 3, HOW MANY APPLES DO YOU HAVE?

_____

4

IN A ROOM, THERE ARE 3 SWITCHES. ONE OF THEM TURNS ON A LIGHT BULB IN ANOTHER ROOM. YOU CAN ENTER THE ROOM WITH THE LIGHT BULB ONLY ONCE. HOW DO YOU FIGURE OUT WHICH SWITCH CONTROLS THE LIGHT BULB?

_____

_____

_____

5

WHAT IS THE QUESTION TO WHICH NO ONE CAN ANSWER "YES"?

_____

6

TWO FATHERS AND TWO SONS GO FISHING. EACH CATCHES ONE FISH, BUT THEY BRING HOME ONLY THREE FISH. HOW IS THIS POSSIBLE?

_____

7

THREE PEOPLE NEED TO CROSS A BRIDGE AT NIGHT WITH ONLY ONE FLASHLIGHT. THE BRIDGE CAN HOLD ONLY TWO PEOPLE AT A TIME, AND SOMEONE MUST ALWAYS CARRY THE FLASHLIGHT. THE FIRST PERSON TAKES 1 MINUTE TO CROSS, THE SECOND TAKES 2 MINUTES, THE THIRD TAKES 5 MINUTES, AND THE FOURTH TAKES 10 MINUTES. HOW DO THEY ALL CROSS IN 17 MINUTES?

_____

_____

_____

_____

8

IN A RACE, IF YOU PASS THE PERSON IN SECOND PLACE, WHAT POSITION ARE YOU IN?

_____

9

A MAN GOES OUT IN THE RAIN WITHOUT AN UMBRELLA OR A HAT, BUT NOT A SINGLE HAIR GETS WET. HOW IS THIS POSSIBLE?

_____

10

IN A ROOM, THERE ARE 4 PEOPLE. EACH PERSON CAN SEE THE OTHER 3. HOW MANY HANDSHAKES OCCUR IF EACH PERSON SHAKES HANDS ONCE WITH EACH OF THE OTHERS?

_____

_____

_____

11

A FARMER NEEDS TO CROSS A RIVER WITH A WOLF, A GOAT, AND A CABBAGE. HE HAS A BOAT BUT CAN TAKE ONLY ONE OTHER AT A TIME. IF HE LEAVES THE WOLF WITH THE GOAT, THE WOLF WILL EAT THE GOAT. IF HE LEAVES THE GOAT WITH THE CABBAGE, THE GOAT WILL EAT THE CABBAGE. HOW CAN HE CROSS THE RIVER WITHOUT ANYONE GETTING EATEN?

_____

_____

_____

12

YOU HAVE 8 IDENTICAL BALLS, BUT ONE IS SLIGHTLY HEAVIER. YOU HAVE A TWO-PAN BALANCE AND CAN MAKE ONLY 2 WEIGHINGS. HOW DO YOU FIND THE HEAVIER BALL?

13

A MAN STANDS BEFORE TWO DOORS. ONE LEADS TO SAFETY, THE OTHER TO DEATH. THERE ARE TWO GUARDS: ONE ALWAYS TELLS THE TRUTH, THE OTHER ALWAYS LIES. THE MAN CAN ASK ONE QUESTION TO ONE GUARD. WHAT QUESTION SHOULD HE ASK TO CHOOSE THE CORRECT DOOR?

SOLUTIONS

1- There is no smoke, it's an electric train.

2- Your name.

3- 3, because you took them.

4- Turn on one switch and wait for a while. Then turn it off and turn on the second switch. Enter the room: if the light bulb is on, it's the second switch; if the light bulb is off but warm, it was the first switch; if it's off and cold, it's the third switch.

5- Are you asleep?

6- They are a grandfather, a father (who is both a father and a son), and a grandson.

7- First, the ones who take 1 and 2 minutes cross (2 minutes), then the one who takes 1 minute returns (3 minutes). The ones who take 5 and 10 minutes cross (13 minutes), the one who takes 2 minutes returns (15 minutes), and finally, the ones who take 1 and 2 minutes cross (17 minutes).

8- You are in second place.

9- He is bald.

10- 6 handshakes (4 people, each shakes hands with 3 others; the count is 4x3/2 to avoid counting the same handshake twice).

11- Take the goat across first. Return alone and take the wolf across, bringing the goat back. Take the cabbage across, then return alone for the goat.

12- Divide the balls into three groups: two groups of 3 and one group of 2. Weigh the two groups of 3. If they are equal, the heavier ball is in the group of 2. If one of the groups is heavier, weigh two of those balls: the heavier one will either be one of the two, or if they balance, it's the third.

13- He should ask one guard, "If I asked the other guard which door leads to safety, what would he say?" Then, he should take the opposite door.

PLAYFUL
RIDDLES

WELCOME TO THE PLAYFUL RIDDLES SECTION, WHERE FUN IS GUARANTEED! HERE YOU'LL FIND RIDDLES THAT PLAY WITH DOUBLE MEANINGS, METAPHORS, AND IRONY, USING LANGUAGE IN A WITTY AND LIGHTHEARTED WAY. EACH RIDDLE IS DESIGNED TO MAKE YOU SMILE WHILE TESTING YOUR CLEVERNESS. GET READY TO LAUGH AND... POOP!

1
IN THE CALENDAR, SOME MONTHS HAVE 30 DAYS, OTHERS 31. HOW MANY MONTHS HAVE 28 DAYS?

_____

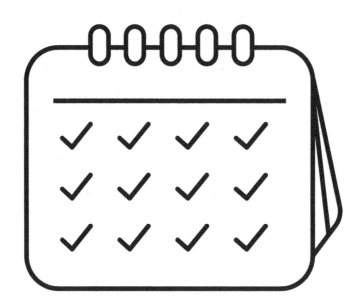

2
IF 1000 KG OF TUNA IS A TON, WHAT ARE 1000 KG OF MARBLE?

_____

3
A BLACK HORSE JUMPS OVER A TOWER AND LANDS ON A SMALL MAN WHO DISAPPEARS. WHAT SCENE IS THIS?

_____

4
IF I HAVE 10 CHOCOLATES AND MATTEO EATS 7, HOW MANY INSULTS DOES MATTEO GET?

_____

5
WHERE DOES THURSDAY COME BEFORE WEDNESDAY?

_____

6
A BLACK DOG IS STANDING IN THE MIDDLE OF AN INTERSECTION, IN A CITY PAINTED ENTIRELY BLACK. THE STREETLIGHTS ARE OUT DUE TO A STORM-CAUSED BLACKOUT. A CAR WITH BROKEN HEADLIGHTS DRIVES TOWARD THE DOG BUT MANAGES TO AVOID IT. HOW DID THE DRIVER SEE THE DOG?

_____

7
WHAT CAN TRAVEL AROUND THE WORLD WHILE STAYING IN A CORNER?

_____

8
WHO DOESN'T RUN AWAY BUT STAYS AT THE SCENE OF THE CRIME?

_____

9
WHAT ANIMAL IS THE BEST AT KEEPING SECRETS?

_____

10
HOW MANY TIMES CAN WE SUBTRACT 10 FROM 100?

_____

11
IN WHICH BATTLE DID NAPOLEON DIE?

_____

12
EVERYONE CAN OPEN IT, BUT NO ONE KNOWS HOW TO CLOSE IT. WHAT IS IT?

_____

SOLUTIONS

1- All of them.

2- A marmalade.

3- A chess game.

4- A lot

5- In the dictionary.

6- It's broad daylight!

7- A stamp.

8- The victim.

9- A fish, because it always keeps its mouth shut.

10- Only once. because after the first subtraction the number is 90.

11- In his last one.

12- An egg.

MATHEMATICAL
RIDDLES

WELCOME TO THE MATHEMATICAL RIDDLES SECTION, WHERE NUMBERS TAKE CENTER STAGE! THESE PUZZLES PLAY WITH CONCEPTS LIKE ADDITION, MULTIPLICATION, PROPORTIONS, AND NUMERICAL LOGIC. EACH RIDDLE CHALLENGES YOU TO REFLECT ON THE PROPERTIES OF NUMBERS AND DO SIMPLE CALCULATIONS, APPLYING LOGICAL REASONING TO FIND THE SOLUTION. GET YOUR BRAIN READY AND PUSH HARD!

1

IF YOU MULTIPLY ANY NUMBER BY ME, THE RESULT WILL ALWAYS BE THE SAME NUMBER. WHO AM I?

_____

2

1. IF YOU SUBTRACT ME FROM YOURSELF, NOTHING CHANGES. WHO AM I?

_____

3

THE SUM OF ME AND MY DOUBLE IS 12. WHO AM I?

_____

4
MOVE A SINGLE STICK TO MAKE THE MATH MAKE SENSE:

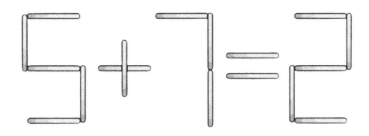

5
A FATHER HAS 4 SONS. EACH OF THEM HAS ONE SISTER. HOW MANY PEOPLE ARE THERE IN TOTAL IN THE FAMILY?

_____

6
WHAT NUMBER, WHEN MULTIPLIED BY ITSELF, GIVES 25?

_____

7
THERE ARE 9 BIRDS ON A TREE. IF YOU SHOOT 3, HOW MANY ARE LEFT ON THE TREE?

_____

8
IF A CLOCK STRIKES 6 CHIMES IN 5 SECONDS, HOW MANY CHIMES WILL IT STRIKE IN 10 SECONDS?

_____

9
WHAT NUMBER BECOMES LESS THAN 9 WHEN YOU FLIP IT?

_____

10
THINK OF A NUMBER. MULTIPLY IT BY 3. ADD 6. DIVIDE THE RESULT BY 3. SUBTRACT THE ORIGINAL NUMBER. WHAT IS THE FINAL RESULT?

_____

11
TWO NUMBERS HAVE A SUM OF 12 AND A PRODUCT OF 35. WHAT ARE THESE NUMBERS?

_____

12
IF ONE AND A HALF HENS LAY ONE AND A HALF EGGS IN ONE AND A HALF DAYS, HOW MANY EGGS DOES ONE HEN LAY IN ONE DAY?

_____

13

A MAN HAS 3 DAUGHTERS. THE PRODUCT OF THEIR AGES IS 36. THE SUM OF THEIR AGES IS THE NUMBER OF THE HOUSE ACROSS THE STREET. KNOWING THE OLDEST DAUGHTER PLAYS THE PIANO, WHAT ARE THEIR AGES?

_____

14

YOU HAVE TWO CONTAINERS: ONE HOLDS 3 LITERS, AND THE OTHER HOLDS 5 LITERS. HOW CAN YOU GET EXACTLY 4 LITERS USING ONLY THESE TWO CONTAINERS AND NO OTHER TOOLS?

_____

15

THERE IS A RIVER WITH TWO PEOPLE ON OPPOSITE SIDES, EACH WITH A PILE OF STONES. THE FIRST PERSON SAYS TO THE SECOND, "GIVE ME ONE OF YOUR STONES, AND I'LL HAVE TWICE AS MANY AS YOU." THE SECOND REPLIES, "GIVE ME ONE OF YOUR STONES, AND WE'LL HAVE THE SAME NUMBER OF STONES." HOW MANY STONES DID THEY EACH START WITH?

_____

SOLUTIONS

1- 1

2- 0

3- 4

4- Move the stick from the "+" sign to make it a "–" and integrate it with the 5 to make it a 9. (9-7=2)

5- The four sons share one sister, so there are 5 children in total, plus the father, making 6 people

6- 5

7- None. After the gunshot, all the birds will fly away

8- There is a time interval between each chime. If 6 chimes take 5 seconds, there will be 11 chimes in 10 seconds, since the first chime doesn't require an interval

9- 9

10- 2

11- 7 and 5

12- 1 egg. If 1.5 hens lay 1.5 eggs in 1.5 days, then one hen lays one egg per day

13- 2, 2, and 9. The ages whose product is 36 come in several combinations, but the clue that the oldest plays the piano rules out combinations where there is no oldest daughter (like 6, 6, 1)

14- Fill the 5-liter container and pour the water into the 3-liter container. You'll have 2 liters left in the 5-liter container. Empty the 3-liter container and pour the 2 liters from the 5-liter container into it. Fill the 5-liter container again and pour water into the 3-liter container until it's full. Now you have exactly 4 liters in the 5-liter container

15- The first person has 7 stones, and the second has 5 If the second person gives one stone to the first, the first person will have 8 stones, and the second will have 4 (double of 4 is 8). If the first person gives one stone to the second, they will both have 6 stones

GENERAL KNOWLEDGE

RIDDLES

WELCOME TO THE GENERAL KNOWLEDGE RIDDLES SECTION, WHERE YOU'LL PUT YOUR KNOWLEDGE OF HISTORY, ART, TRADITIONS, AND GLOBAL CURIOSITIES TO THE TEST. FROM FAMOUS AUTHORS TO HISTORICAL EVENTS, THESE RIDDLES WILL CHALLENGE YOUR UNDERSTANDING OF THE WORLD AND KEEP YOU ENTERTAINED. GET READY TO EXPLORE THE RICH CULTURAL HERITAGE OF THE WORLD... WHILE YOU POOP!

1

I WAS GUIDED BY VIRGIL AND MET BEATRICE DURING A JOURNEY THROUGH HELL, PURGATORY, AND PARADISE. WHO AM I?

_____

2

I WAS BORN IN VINCI AND PAINTED AN ENIGMATIC SMILE THAT HAS FASCINATED THE WORLD. WHO AM I?

_____

3

I WAS THE LEADER OF A GREAT EMPIRE, ASSASSINATED BY THOSE I TRUSTED. I CROSSED THE RUBICON AND UTTERED THE WORDS "ET TU, BRUTE?" WHO AM I?

_____

4

I SAILED ACROSS THE ATLANTIC IN 1492, DISCOVERING A NEW WORLD. WHO AM I?

_____

5

I PROPOSED THE THEORY OF RELATIVITY, WHICH CHANGED THE WAY WE UNDERSTAND SPACE AND TIME. WHO AM I?

_____

6

I AM A FAMOUS PLAYWRIGHT KNOWN FOR MY TRAGEDIES, COMEDIES, AND HISTORIES. MY WORKS HAVE BEEN PERFORMED FOR CENTURIES. WHO AM I?

_____

7

I AM A MONUMENTAL STATUE GIVEN TO THE UNITED STATES BY FRANCE, SYMBOLIZING FREEDOM AND DEMOCRACY. WHO AM I?

_____

8

I DISCOVERED THE LAW OF GRAVITY AFTER WATCHING AN APPLE FALL FROM A TREE. WHO AM I?

_____

9

I AM KNOWN FOR MY THEORY OF EVOLUTION, AND I WROTE ON THE ORIGIN OF SPECIES. WHO AM I?

_____

10
I WAS THE FIRST PRESIDENT OF THE UNITED STATES, LEADING MY COUNTRY TO INDEPENDENCE. WHO AM I?

_____

11
I AM THE CITY WHERE THE FAMOUS EIFFEL TOWER STANDS. WHAT CITY AM I?

_____

12
I COMPOSED THE FIFTH SYMPHONY AND CONTINUED TO CREATE MUSIC EVEN AFTER BECOMING DEAF. WHO AM I?

_____

COMPLETE THE SENTENCES

"I HAVE A ____." "THAT ONE DAY THIS NATION WILL ____ AND LIVE OUT THE TRUE MEANING OF ITS CREED."

"THE JOURNEY OF A THOUSAND MILES BEGINS ____ A SINGLE STEP."

"AN EYE FOR AN EYE LEAVES ____ THE WHOLE WORLD ____."

"THE ONLY THING WE HAVE TO FEAR IS FEAR ____."

"GIVE A MAN A FISH, AND YOU FEED HIM ____ A DAY; TEACH A MAN TO FISH, AND YOU FEED HIM FOR ____."

"IT ALWAYS SEEMS IMPOSSIBLE ____ IT'S DONE."

"TO BE, OR ____ TO BE, ____ IS THE QUESTION."

"THAT'S ONE SMALL STEP FOR ____, ONE GIANT ____ FOR MANKIND."

"HE WHO HAS A WHY TO LIVE ____ BEAR ALMOST ANY ____."

"INJUSTICE ANYWHERE IS A THREAT TO ____ EVERYWHERE."

SOLUTIONS

1- Dante Alighieri.

2- Leonardo da Vinci.

3- Julius Caesar.

4- Christopher Columbus.

5- Albert Einstein.

6- William Shakespeare.

7- The Statue of Liberty.

8- Isaac Newton.

9- Charles Darwin.

10- George Washington.

11- Paris.

12- Ludwig van Beethoven.

SENTENCES

Dream, rise. (Part of Martin Luther King Jr.'s I Have a Dream speech)

With. (A famous Chinese proverb by Lao Tzu, emphasizing the importance of taking the first step)

Both, blind. (A famous quote by Mahatma Gandhi, warning against the cycle of revenge)

Itself. (Franklin D. Roosevelt's famous statement during his inaugural address)

For, life. (A proverb about self-sufficiency and the value of teaching skills)

Until. (A famous quote by Nelson Mandela, encouraging perseverance)

Not, that. (A famous line from Shakespeare's Hamlet)

Man, leap. (Neil Armstrong's words when he became the first person to walk on the moon)

Can, how. (Friedrich Nietzsche's quote about the importance of purpose)

Justice. (Martin Luther King Jr.'s statement on the interconnectedness of justice)

LOGICAL-DEDUCTIVE

PUZZLES

WELCOME TO THE LOGICAL-DEDUCTIVE PUZZLES SECTION, WHERE DEDUCTION AND RIGOROUS REASONING ARE THE KEYS TO REACHING THE SOLUTION. THESE PUZZLES REQUIRE LOGICAL THINKING SEQUENCES AND DEDUCTIVE STEPS TO SOLVE COMPLEX PROBLEMS, JUST LIKE SHERLOCK HOLMES WOULD WITH HIS CLUES. TEST YOURSELF, FOLLOW EVERY CLUE, AND UNCOVER THE TRUTH BEHIND EACH MYSTERY!

1

A MAN LIVES ON THE 12TH FLOOR OF A BUILDING. EVERY DAY, HE TAKES THE ELEVATOR TO THE GROUND FLOOR TO GO TO WORK. WHEN HE RETURNS, HE ONLY TAKES THE ELEVATOR TO THE 10TH FLOOR AND THEN WALKS UP THE STAIRS TO THE 12TH. WHY?

_____

2

A KING DECIDES TO REWARD THE SUBJECT WHO TELLS HIM THE MOST "CLEVER" LIE WITH A LARGE SUM OF MONEY. DOZENS OF PEOPLE COME FORWARD: SOME CLAIM THEY HAVE BEEN TO THE MOON, OTHERS THAT THEY CAN WALK THROUGH FIRE WITHOUT BURNING. HOWEVER, NONE OF THESE LIES SATISFY THE KING. FINALLY, A VERY POOR FARMER ARRIVES AND, AFTER HEARING HIS STORY, THE KING GIVES HIM THE PRIZE. WHAT DID THE FARMER SAY?

_____

3

A MAN WAS BORN ON DECEMBER 25TH, BUT HE CELEBRATES HIS BIRTHDAY IN THE SUMMER. HOW IS THIS POSSIBLE?

_____

4

A WOMAN BUYS A PARROT, BUT AFTER A WEEK, SHE COMPLAINS THAT THE BIRD HASN'T SPOKEN A SINGLE WORD. THE SHOPKEEPER INSISTS THAT THE PARROT CAN SPEAK. WHY HASN'T IT SPOKEN?

5

A MAN ENTERS A STORE AND STEALS A €100 BILL FROM THE CASH REGISTER. HE THEN RETURNS AND BUYS AN ITEM WORTH €70, PAYING WITH THE STOLEN €100 BILL. THE SHOPKEEPER GIVES HIM €30 IN CHANGE. HOW MUCH DID THE SHOPKEEPER LOSE IN TOTAL?

6

THREE BOXES EACH CONTAIN TWO BALLS. ONE BOX HAS TWO RED BALLS, ONE HAS TWO WHITE BALLS, AND THE THIRD HAS ONE RED BALL AND ONE WHITE BALL. THE BOXES ARE LABELED, BUT ALL THE LABELS ARE WRONG. HOW CAN YOU DETERMINE WHAT IS IN EACH BOX BY PICKING ONLY ONE BALL?

7

A MAN IS LOOKING AT A PORTRAIT. SOMEONE ASKS HIM WHO THE PERSON IN THE PICTURE IS. THE MAN REPLIES, "BROTHERS AND SISTERS, I HAVE NONE, BUT THE FATHER OF THIS MAN IS THE SON OF MY FATHER." WHO IS THE MAN IN THE PORTRAIT?

_____

8

THERE ARE 12 COINS, ALL IDENTICAL IN WEIGHT EXCEPT FOR ONE, WHICH IS EITHER SLIGHTLY HEAVIER OR LIGHTER. YOU HAVE A TWO-PAN BALANCE AND CAN MAKE ONLY THREE WEIGHINGS. HOW DO YOU IDENTIFY THE DIFFERENT COIN AND DETERMINE IF IT IS HEAVIER OR LIGHTER?

_____

_____

_____

_____

9

THERE ARE THREE MEN IN A ROOM. ONE OF THEM IS A MURDERER. THE FIRST MAN SAYS, "I AM NOT THE MURDERER." THE SECOND MAN SAYS, "THE FIRST MAN IS TELLING THE TRUTH." THE THIRD MAN SAYS, "I AM THE MURDERER." IF ONLY ONE OF THEM IS TELLING THE TRUTH, WHO IS THE MURDERER?

_____

10

IN A ROOM THERE ARE TWO PEOPLE. A FATHER, WHO IS 45 YEARS OLD, AND A SON WHO IS 50. HOW IS THIS POSSIBLE?

_____

11

LUCA ALTERNATES BETWEEN TELLING THE TRUTH AND LYING (EVERY TRUE STATEMENT IS FOLLOWED BY A FALSE ONE, AND VICE VERSA). WHICH OF THE FOLLOWING STATEMENTS CAN BE ATTRIBUTED TO LUCA?

A) BOTH OF MY STATEMENTS ARE FALSE
B) THIS STATEMENT IS FALSE
C) MY PREVIOUS STATEMENT IS FALSE
D) MY PREVIOUS STATEMENT IS TRUE
E) MY PREVIOUS AND NEXT STATEMENTS ARE TRUE

12

IN A COUNTRY WHERE ALL INHABITANTS ARE THIEVES, NOTHING CAN BE LEFT IN THE STREET WITHOUT BEING STOLEN. THE ONLY WAY TO SEND SOMETHING WITHOUT IT BEING STOLEN IS TO PLACE IT IN A LOCKED SAFE, WHICH IS THE ONLY THING THIEVES WON'T STEAL. AT BIRTH, EACH INHABITANT RECEIVES A SAFE AND A LOCK, AND THEY POSSESS THE ONLY KEY TO THEIR LOCK. EACH SAFE CAN BE CLOSED WITH MULTIPLE LOCKS, BUT THE KEY CANNOT BE PASSED ON OR TAKEN OUT OF THE HOUSE, AS IT WOULD BE STOLEN. FURTHERMORE, NO COPIES OF THE KEYS CAN BE MADE. HOW CAN SOMEONE SEND A BIRTHDAY GIFT TO A FRIEND IN THIS COUNTRY?

_____

_____

_____

_____

_____

SOLUTIONS

1- The man is too short to reach the button for the 12th floor, so he presses the 10th and walks the rest of the way.

2- The farmer said that the king's late father owed him a great sum of money. If the king admits it's a lie, he must pay him the sum; if he accepts it as truth, he must pay the debt.

3- The man lives in the southern hemisphere, where December 25th falls in summer.

4- The parrot is deaf.

5- €100. The shopkeeper lost the €100 that was initially stolen, and the €70 item and €30 change simply compensated for the stolen bill.

6- Take a ball from the box labeled "red and white." Since the label is wrong, if you pick a red ball, that box contains only red balls. You can then deduce the contents of the other boxes.

7- The man's son. The man says that the father of the person in the picture is the son of his father, meaning he is talking about his own son.

8- Divide the coins into three groups of 4. Weigh two groups at a time. If they balance, the odd coin is in the group not weighed; otherwise, it's in one of the two groups weighed. Repeat the process with the suspicious group until the odd coin is found.

9- The second man is the murderer. If the third man were the murderer, there would be two truths. If the first man is lying, then the second man is also lying when he says the first man is telling the truth, meaning the second man must be the murderer.

10- He isn't his biological son. The man could be a father, but the person in the room isn't his child!

11- C) My previous statement is false. If Luca alternates between true and false statements, "My previous statement is false" must be true for the alternation to work.

12- The sender locks the safe with their own lock and sends it. The recipient adds their lock and sends it back to the sender, who removes their lock. The safe is then returned to the recipient, who unlocks it with their key.

LINGUISTIC

PUZZLES

WELCOME TO THE LINGUISTIC PUZZLES SECTION, WHERE WORDS BECOME A TRUE BRAIN TEASER! HERE YOU'LL FIND GAMES BASED ON ANAGRAMS, LOGOGRIPHS, AND OTHER CHALLENGES THAT TEST YOUR ABILITY TO MANIPULATE AND REORGANIZE LETTERS AND WORDS. GET READY TO EXPLORE THE RICHNESS OF LANGUAGE AND DISCOVER NEW PERSPECTIVES THROUGH EACH PUZZLE!

GIVEN A WORD, FIND AS MANY ANAGRAMS AS POSSIBLE:

1
PEACH

_____

_____

_____

_____

_____

_____

2
DREAM

_____

_____

_____

_____

_____

3
HONEY

_____

_____

_____

_____

_____

_____

4
WIND

_____

_____

_____

_____

5
ANNA WHITE

_____

_____

_____

_____

_____

_____

_____

_____

_____

_____

WELCOME TO THE SUB-SECTION OF METAGRAMS, A FASCINATING WORD GAME WHERE YOU START WITH ONE WORD AND, BY CHANGING ONE LETTER AT A TIME, YOU REACH ANOTHER WORD. IN THIS CASE, NOT EVERY INTERMEDIATE STEP NEEDS TO FORM A MEANINGFUL WORD; THE REAL GOAL IS TO REACH THE FINAL SOLUTION WITH AS FEW CHANGES AS POSSIBLE. CHALLENGE YOURSELF AND SEE HOW MANY TRANSFORMATIONS AND HOW MUCH POOP YOU CAN DO!

GIVEN THE WORD, PERFORM THE METAGRAM:

1

START: HAND
END: FOOT

_____

_____

_____

_____

_____

2

START: COLD
END: WARM

_____

_____

_____

_____

_____

3

START: HEAD
END: TAIL

_____

_____

_____

_____

_____

_____

4

START: FAST
END: SLOW

_____

_____

_____

_____

5

START: BEAR
END: LION

_____

_____

_____

6

START: FIRE
END: COAL

_____

_____

_____

_____

7

START: NOTE
END: SONG

_____

_____

_____

_____

_____

8

START: MOON
END: STAR

_____

_____

_____

_____

_____

SOLUTIONS

1- Each, Ape, Cap, Pace, Sap, Ace

2- Read, Dare, Red, Made, Arm, Ear

3- One, Hey, Hen, Yen, No, Hoe

4- Win, Din, Wit, End

5- Anna, What, White, Wine, Hint, Tina, Hat, Thin, Tan, New, Wait

METAGRAMS

1- HAND, HOND, HOOD, FOOD, FOOT

2- COLD, WOLD, WORD, WARD, WARM

3- HEAD, HEAL, TEAL, TAAL, TAIL

4- FAST, SAST, SASW, SAOW, SLOW

5- BEAR, LEAR, LIAR, LIAN, LION

6- FIRE, FARL, CARL, COAL

7- NOTE, NOME, SOME, SONE, SONG

8- MOON, MORN, SORN, SARN, STAR

GEOMETRIC

PUZZLES

WELCOME TO THE GEOMETRIC PUZZLES SECTION, WHERE FIGURES, SHAPES, AND SPATIAL MOVEMENTS ARE AT THE HEART OF THE CHALLENGES. THESE PUZZLES REQUIRE SPATIAL AND GEOMETRIC THINKING, FINDING SOLUTIONS BY OBSERVING THE PROPERTIES OF SHAPES. GET READY TO VISUALIZE AND SOLVE PROBLEMS WHERE GEOMETRY BECOMES AN INTRIGUING AND EXCITING GAME— IT'S KIND OF LIKE POOPING.

1
IS IT POSSIBLE TO FIT 101 SQUARES, EACH 10 METERS PER SIDE, ON A SQUARE THAT IS 108 METERS PER SIDE WITHOUT CUTTING ANY OF THEM?

2
TWO CASTAWAYS MANAGE TO FILL A CYLINDRICAL BUCKET WITH RAINWATER TO THE BRIM DURING A STORM. NOW, THEY WANT TO DIVIDE THE WATER EQUALLY BETWEEN THEM, BUT THEY ONLY HAVE THE BUCKET OF WATER AND AN EMPTY PLASTIC BAG. HOW CAN THEY SPLIT THE WATER EVENLY WITHOUT ANY MEASURING TOOLS?

3

A MAN HAD FOUR SONS, AND ONE OF THEM ASKED FOR HIS INHERITANCE EARLY. THE FATHER GAVE HIM A QUARTER OF HIS LANDS. (SEE THE FIGURE). THE SON WASTED ALL HIS INHERITANCE. AFTER MANY YEARS, WHEN THE FATHER WANTED TO DIVIDE THE REMAINING LAND AMONG HIS OTHER THREE SONS, A BOY WHO WAS THE SON OF THE FIRST SON APPEARED. THE OLD MAN SAID, "THIS BOY IS STILL PART OF THE FAMILY, AND I WILL ENSURE THAT HE GETS AN EQUAL SHARE OF THE REMAINING LAND, JUST LIKE HIS UNCLES." HOW DID THE FATHER DIVIDE THE LAND?

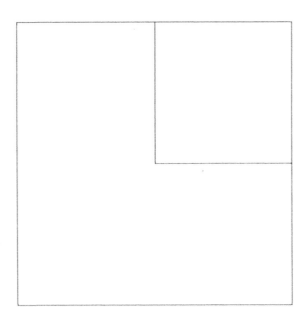

4

AT A WOODWORKING COMPANY, ROSEWOOD CUBES MEASURING 50 CENTIMETERS ON EACH SIDE ARRIVE AND NEED TO BE CUT INTO 10-CENTIMETER CUBES. UNFORTUNATELY, THE LAST SHIPMENT ARRIVED DAMAGED ON ALL ITS FACES DUE TO SEA CORROSION. AFTER COMPLETING THE CUTTING PROCESS, HOW MANY PERFECT CUBES CAN BE OBTAINED, AND HOW MANY WILL BE DAMAGED ON ONE OR MORE FACES?

5
WHICH IS THE CORRECT IMAGE THAT CORRESPONDS TO THE CUBE AT THE TOP?

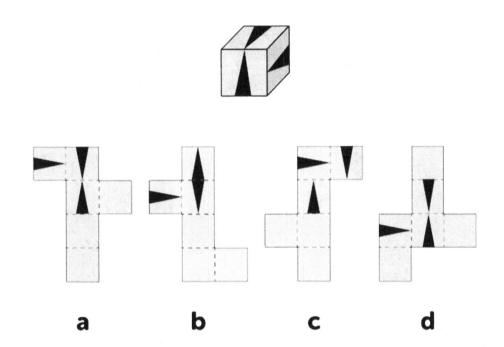

a   b   c   d

SOLUTIONS

1- 100 squares can be arranged to leave two central corridors, each 8 meters wide. The 101st square can fit if rotated 45°.

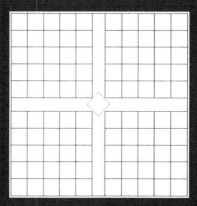

2- Pour the water from the cylindrical bucket into the plastic bag until the bucket is tilted and the remaining water forms the diagonal of the cylinder, ensuring an equal split.

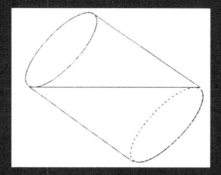

3- Divide the land as follows:

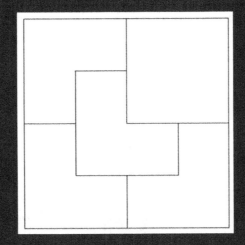

4- From the 50 cm cube, cut into 125 cubes of 10 cm, resulting in:

27 perfect cubes,
8 cubes damaged on three faces,
36 cubes damaged on two faces,
54 cubes damaged on one face.

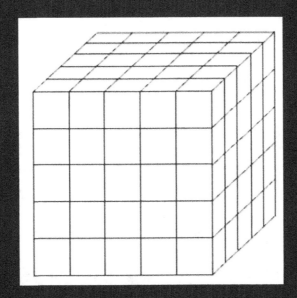

5- Number A.

PHILOSOPHICAL

PUZZLES

WELCOME TO THE PHILOSOPHICAL PUZZLES SECTION, WHERE ABSTRACT THINKING TAKES OVER. THESE PUZZLES CHALLENGE YOU TO REFLECT ON PARADOXES, DILEMMAS, AND METAPHYSICAL CONCEPTS, TESTING YOUR ABILITY FOR DEEP REASONING AND HOW YOU PERCEIVE REALITY. THE ANSWERS EXPLORE DIFFERENT ASPECTS OF PHILOSOPHICAL PUZZLES, BUT OFTEN THERE ARE NO DEFINITIVE SOLUTIONS, AS EVERYTHING DEPENDS ON PHILOSOPHICAL PERSPECTIVE AND CONCEPTUAL CONTEXT. THEY ARE PERFECT TOOLS FOR STIMULATING CRITICAL THINKING AND PERSONAL REFLECTION! BECAUSE REFLECTING WHILE POOPING IS ALWAYS A GOOD IDEA.

1
"IF A TREE FALLS IN A FOREST AND NO ONE IS AROUND TO HEAR IT, DOES IT MAKE A SOUND?"

_____

_____

_____

2
"CAN A SINGLE ACTION BE BOTH RIGHT AND WRONG AT THE SAME TIME?"

_____

_____

_____

3
"IF TIME DIDN'T EXIST, WHAT WOULD CHANGE IN THE WORLD?"

_____

_____

_____

_____

4
"IF YOU STOP THINKING ABOUT YOURSELF, DO YOU STILL EXIST?"

_____

_____

_____

_____

5
"IF YOU LIE ABOUT A LIE, ARE YOU TELLING THE TRUTH?"

_____

_____

_____

_____

6
"CAN GOOD EXIST WITHOUT EVIL?"

_____

_____

_____

_____

7
"CAN A PERSON TRULY BE FREE IF THEIR ACTIONS ARE DETERMINED BY THEIR PAST?"

_____

_____

_____

_____

8
"IF AN ARTIFICIAL BEING BECOMES CONSCIOUS, IS IT ALIVE?"

_____

_____

_____

_____

9
"IF GOD IS OMNIPOTENT, CAN HE CREATE A ROCK SO HEAVY THAT EVEN HE CANNOT LIFT IT?"

_____

_____

_____

_____

10
"IF EVERY PART OF YOUR BODY IS REPLACED, ARE YOU STILL THE SAME PERSON?"

_____

_____

_____

_____

11
"WHAT IS MORE REAL: THE PRESENT, THE PAST, OR THE FUTURE?"

_____

_____

_____

_____

12
"CAN SOMETHING EXIST WITHOUT A CAUSE?"

_____

_____

_____

_____

CONSIDERATIONS

1
Yes, scientifically speaking, sound is a vibration that propagates through the air, so the tree would still make a sound even if no one is there to hear it. However, philosophically, sound exists only if there's a being capable of perceiving it, so without an observer, "sound" becomes a matter of perception rather than objective existence.

2
Yes, the same action can be seen as right or wrong depending on context, culture, morality, and consequences. For example, theft is generally considered morally wrong, but if it is done to save a life, it might be seen as justified from another perspective.

3
Without time, the concept of change and movement would disappear. There would be no evolution, growth, or decay. Everything would be static. However, time could be a mental construct humans use to better understand reality, so without time, we might perceive everything differently, but existence would continue in some form.

4

According to Descartes, "Cogito, ergo sum" (I think, therefore I am) suggests that self-awareness proves existence. However, we exist independently of thinking actively about ourselves. Our body, our physical being, exists even when we are unconscious or not reflecting on ourselves.

5

If you lie about a lie, you are technically correcting false information, so it could be considered the truth. However, the concept is paradoxical: truth cannot emerge from a lie, so despite the appearance of truth, it remains a logical puzzle.

6

Philosophically, the concept of "good" needs "evil" for it to be understood, as the two ideas are complementary. Without evil, there would be no benchmark for defining what is good. However, there is a theory that good is intrinsic and that evil is simply a distortion of good.

7

If we accept that past experiences influence our choices, it seems that freedom is limited. However, freedom could lie in our ability to reflect on these influences and make conscious choices. Free will may exist despite the influence of the past, as we can choose to overcome our circumstances.

8

If we define life in biological terms, a conscious artificial being is not alive because it lacks the biological characteristics of living organisms. However, if consciousness is the criterion for defining life, then it could be considered "alive" in a broader sense, as a form of artificial life.

9

This is a classic paradox questioning the logical coherence of omnipotence. One answer could be that omnipotence, to be consistent, does not imply the ability to do the impossible or absurd. God cannot create logical contradictions, so the question is flawed.

10

Philosophically, this is the "Ship of Theseus" paradox. The answer depends on how we define identity. If we identify with our mind and memory, then we might still be the same person. However, if we identify with the physical body, then perhaps not. Personally, I think identity is more linked to the continuity of consciousness than to physicality.

11

The present is the only moment we perceive directly, so it seems more "real." However, the past has left tangible traces, and the future, although uncertain, exists in our thoughts and expectations. We could say that all three exist in different ways.

12

According to the principle of causality, every effect must have a cause. However, in some areas of quantum physics, random events appear to have no direct cause. This suggests that causality might not be a universal law but rather a feature of our macroscopic universe.

PRACTICAL

PUZZLES

WELCOME TO THE PRACTICAL PUZZLES SECTION, WHERE LOGIC MEETS PHYSICS AND MECHANICS TO SOLVE REAL-WORLD PROBLEMS. THESE PUZZLES REQUIRE CLEVER SOLUTIONS BASED ON THE USE OF TOOLS OR SOLVING REAL-LIFE SITUATIONS. GET READY TO TEST YOUR PRACTICAL REASONING AND YOUR ABILITY TO FIND SOLUTIONS TO REAL-WORLD CHALLENGES!

1
IF YOU DROP A RUBBER BALL FROM A HEIGHT OF 10 METERS, EACH TIME IT BOUNCES, IT REACHES 80% OF THE PREVIOUS HEIGHT. HOW HIGH WILL IT BOUNCE ON THE SECOND REBOUND?

_____

2
IF YOU HAVE A GLASS OF WATER WITH ICE INSIDE, WILL THE WATER LEVEL RISE OR FALL ONCE THE ICE MELTS?

_____

3
IF YOU HAVE A ROPE 1 METER LONG AND YOU FOLD IT IN HALF, AND THEN FOLD IT IN HALF AGAIN, HOW LONG WILL THE ROPE BE AFTER THE SECOND FOLD?

_____

4

IF YOU HAVE A LADDER LEANING AGAINST A WALL AND IT STARTS SLIDING SLOWLY DOWNWARD, WHAT HAPPENS TO ITS ANGLE OF INCLINATION WITH THE WALL?

_____

5

IF YOU PUT A POT OF WATER ON THE STOVE AND COVER IT WITH A LID, WILL THE WATER BOIL FASTER OR SLOWER COMPARED TO A POT WITHOUT A LID?

_____

6

TWO CARS START AT THE SAME TIME IN OPPOSITE DIRECTIONS ON A STRAIGHT ROAD. ONE CAR TRAVELS TWICE AS FAST AS THE OTHER. HOW LONG WILL IT TAKE THEM TO BE 300 KM APART IF THE SLOWER CAR TRAVELS AT 60 KM/H?

_____

_____

_____

7

YOU HAVE TWO PIECES OF ROPE, AND EACH TAKES EXACTLY ONE HOUR TO BURN COMPLETELY. HOWEVER, THE ROPES DO NOT BURN EVENLY—ONE HALF MIGHT BURN FASTER THAN THE OTHER. HOW CAN YOU MEASURE EXACTLY 45 MINUTES USING JUST THESE TWO ROPES AND A LIGHTER?

8

YOU HAVE A BARREL THAT CONTAINS EXACTLY 40 LITERS OF WATER, AND YOU NEED TO KNOW IF THE BARREL IS HALF FULL WITHOUT USING ANY MEASURING TOOLS. HOW DO YOU DO IT?

9

YOU ARE IN A ROOM, AND IN FRONT OF YOU IS A LARGE STONE, SO HEAVY THAT IT SEEMS IMPOSSIBLE TO LIFT WITH JUST YOUR STRENGTH. IN THE ROOM, YOU HAVE ONLY A LONG WOODEN ROD AND A LARGE ROCK. THE STONE MUST BE MOVED WITHIN A FEW MINUTES, BUT YOU HAVE NO OTHER EQUIPMENT AVAILABLE.
QUESTION: HOW CAN YOU LIFT THE STONE, USING THE AVAILABLE TOOLS, WITHOUT EXCEEDING YOUR PHYSICAL STRENGTH?

SOLUTIONS

1- On the second bounce, the ball will reach 64% of the original height (80% of 80%). So, it will bounce to 6.4 meters.

2- The water level will remain the same. The ice, while floating, displaces an amount of water equal to its weight. When it melts, it exactly fills the space it had displaced.

3- After the second fold, the rope will be 25 cm long.

4- The angle of inclination decreases as the ladder slides down.

5- The water will boil faster with the lid on. The lid reduces heat loss and traps the steam, increasing the pressure and heat inside the pot.

6- The faster car travels at 120 km/h (twice the speed of 60 km/h). Combined, they travel at 180 km/h. To cover 300 km, it will take 300 ÷ 180 = 1.67 hours, or about 1 hour and 40 minutes.

7- Light the first rope from both ends and the second rope from one end. The first rope will burn completely in 30 minutes (since it's burning from both ends), and the second will burn from one end in 30 minutes. Once the first rope has burned, light the other end of the second rope. This remaining part will now burn in 15 minutes. In total, you will have measured 45 minutes.

8- Tilt the barrel until the water reaches the edge of the barrel. If the bottom of the barrel is still covered by water while tilting, then the barrel is half full. If the bottom is not covered, it contains less than half.

9- You can lift the stone using the principle of the lever. Place the large rock near the stone to act as a fulcrum. Then use the wooden rod as a lever: place one end under the stone and push down on the other end of the rod. This will apply the physical principle of the lever, allowing you to lift a much heavier object with less force, provided the lever is long enough.

SEQUENCE

PUZZLES

① ② ③

④ ⑤ ⑥

⑦ ⑧ ⑨

WELCOME TO THE SEQUENCE PUZZLES SECTION, WHERE THE TASK IS TO DISCOVER THE RULE OR PATTERN THAT CONNECTS NUMBERS, LETTERS, OR SYMBOLS. EACH PUZZLE CHALLENGES YOU TO IDENTIFY THE HIDDEN LOGIC BEHIND A SERIES, REQUIRING ATTENTION TO DETAIL AND THE ABILITY TO RECOGNIZE PATTERNS. TEST YOUR INTUITION AND SOLVE THE SEQUENCES THAT LIE BEHIND THESE FASCINATING CHALLENGES!

1

2, 4, 8, 16, 32, ?

2

1.1, 4, 9, 16, 25, ?

3

1, 1, 2, 3, 5, 8, 13, ?

4
WHICH SHAPE COMES AFTER THE BLACK TRIANGLE?

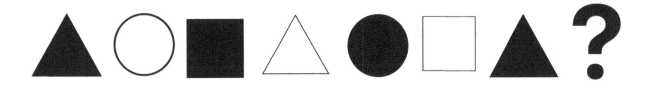

_____

5

3, 6, 11, 18, 27, ?

_____

6

5, 10, 20, 40, ?

_____

7

A, C, F, J, O, ?

8

CIRCLE THE RECTANGLE THAT COMPLETES THE SEQUENCE:

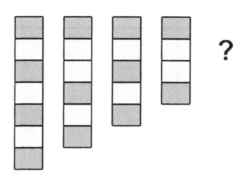

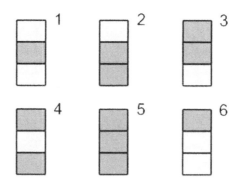

9

8, 6, 7, 5, 6, 4, 5, ?

10

B, E, H, K, N, ?

11

12 ... 6
10 ... 5
8 ... 4
6 ... 3
2 ... ?

(THE ANSWER IS NOT ONE)

12

?, 3, 8, 63, 3968

_____

13

3, 6, 12, 21, 33, ?

_____

14

CIRCLE THE FIGURE THAT IS NOT IN LINE WITH THE OTHERS:

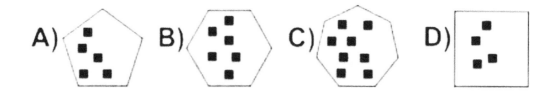

SOLUTIONS

1- 64 (each number is double the previous one).

2- 36 (these are squares of 1, 2, 3, 4, 5, 6).

3- 21 (this is the Fibonacci sequence: each number is the sum of the previous two).

4- The empty circle. The geometric shapes are positioned cyclically here: triangle, circle, and square.

5- 38 (the difference between the numbers increases by 2).

6- 80 (each number is double the previous one).

7- U (alphabetic jumps increase by 1: A+2=C, +3=F, +4=J, +5=O, +6=U).

8- 4. Here, the top two rectangles do not change. With each move to the right, the third rectangle is removed, while the bottom cells shift upwards by one step.

9- 3 (alternating between -2 and -1).

10- Q (skipping three letters).

11- The answer is 2. That is the number of letters the words "twelve" "ten" etc. have.

12- Each number is the square of the next, minus 1.

13- You add 3, 6, 9, 12 etc., to the previous number.

14- C. Because it contains eight squares but has 7 sides.

COMBINATORIAL

LOGIC PUZZLES

WELCOME TO THE COMBINATORIAL LOGIC PUZZLES SECTION, WHERE THE TASK IS TO FIND THE CORRECT COMBINATION OF EVENTS OR CONDITIONS. THESE PUZZLES WILL CHALLENGE YOU, JUST LIKE CLASSIC PUZZLES WITH MULTIPLE VARIABLES, REQUIRING ATTENTION AND DEDUCTION TO SOLVE COMPLEX SITUATIONS. GET READY TO FIT ALL THE PIECES TOGETHER AND DISCOVER THE FINAL SOLUTION BEFORE YOU FINISH POOPING!

1

THREE PEOPLE ARE WEARING EITHER A RED OR BLUE HAT. THEY CANNOT SEE THEIR OWN HAT BUT CAN SEE THE OTHERS' HATS. THEY KNOW THERE ARE AT LEAST TWO RED HATS. IF ONE PERSON SEES TWO RED HATS ON THE OTHERS, WHAT COLOR IS THEIR HAT?

2

AT A DINNER, THERE ARE FOUR PEOPLE, EACH WITH DIFFERENT FOOD PREFERENCES. WHO EATS WHAT IF: PERSON A DOESN'T EAT FISH, PERSON B EATS ONLY MEAT, PERSON C HATES VEGETABLES, AND PERSON D IS A VEGETARIAN?

3

FIVE FRIENDS ARE SITTING IN A CIRCLE. EACH HAS EITHER AN EVEN OR ODD NUMBER, BUT THEY CANNOT SEE THEIR OWN NUMBER. ONLY THOSE WITH AN EVEN NUMBER CAN CHANGE PLACES. HOW CAN THEY ALL SIT IN INCREASING ORDER?

4

THERE ARE THREE BOXES: ONE CONTAINS ONLY
APPLES, ONE CONTAINS ONLY ORANGES, AND ONE
CONTAINS BOTH. EACH BOX HAS AN INCORRECT LABEL.
HOW DO YOU DETERMINE WHAT'S IN EACH BOX IF YOU
CAN ONLY TAKE ONE FRUIT FROM ONE BOX?

_____

_____

_____

5

YOU HAVE TWO HOURGLASSES—ONE MEASURES 4
MINUTES, AND THE OTHER MEASURES 7 MINUTES. HOW
DO YOU MEASURE EXACTLY 9 MINUTES?

_____

_____

_____

6

YOU HAVE 6 GLASSES LINED UP IN A ROW. THE FIRST
THREE ARE FULL OF WATER, WHILE THE LAST THREE ARE
EMPTY. YOU NEED TO ALTERNATE FULL AND EMPTY
GLASSES, BUT YOU CAN ONLY TOUCH ONE GLASS. HOW
DO YOU DO IT?

_____

_____

_____

7

THERE ARE THREE PEOPLE, EACH WITH A DIFFERENT PET: A DOG, A CAT, AND A HAMSTER. YOU KNOW THAT:

- LAURA DOES NOT OWN THE HAMSTER.
- THE PERSON WHO OWNS THE DOG IS JULIA'S NEIGHBOR.
- ROBERTO LIVES ACROSS THE STREET FROM THE PERSON WHO OWNS THE CAT.

WHO OWNS WHICH PET?

_____

_____

_____

8

YOU HAVE 5 TICKETS NUMBERED FROM 1 TO 5. YOU NEED TO DISTRIBUTE THEM TO 5 PEOPLE IN SUCH A WAY THAT NO ONE RECEIVES THE TICKET WITH THEIR OWN NUMBER. WHAT IS THE MAXIMUM NUMBER OF PEOPLE WHO CAN RECEIVE THE WRONG TICKET?

_____

_____

_____

SOLUTIONS

1- Red, because there are at least two red hats and they already see two red ones on the others.

2- A eats meat, B eats meat, C eats fish, and D eats vegetables.

3- By gradually swapping places, only those with even numbers, until the sequence is ordered.

4- Take a fruit from the box labeled "mixed." Since all labels are wrong, if you pick an apple, that box contains only apples. Then you can relabel the other boxes accordingly.

5- Start both hourglasses. When the 4-minute hourglass runs out, flip it over immediately. When the 7-minute hourglass runs out, flip it as well. When the 4-minute hourglass runs out again, exactly 9 minutes will have passed.

6- Take the second full glass (glass number 2) and pour its contents into glass number 5, which is empty. Now the sequence is alternated: full, empty, full, empty, full, empty.

7- Laura owns the dog, Roberto owns the hamster, Julia owns the cat.

8- All 5 people can receive the wrong ticket. This is an example of a "derangement" (a permutation where no element is in its correct position). It is possible to distribute all the tickets so that no one gets their own number.

CURIOSITIES
AND PARADOXES

WELCOME TO THE CURIOSITIES AND PARADOXES SECTION, DESIGNED TO ENTERTAIN YOU WITH FASCINATING QUESTIONS AND PARADOXES WHILE YOU TAKE A BREAK... PERFECT FOR WHEN YOU'RE IN THE BATHROOM! HERE, YOU'LL DISCOVER INTERESTING FACTS AND STIMULATE YOUR MIND WITH REFLECTIONS THAT CHALLENGE LOGIC AND COMMON SENSE. GET READY TO HAVE FUN AND LEARN SOMETHING NEW, EVEN DURING MOMENTS OF RELAXATION!

1

DO YOU KNOW WHICH WAS THE FIRST PIZZERIA OPENED IN THE WORLD?

A) PIZZA HUT
B) PIZZERIA BRANDI
C) ANTICA PIZZERIA PORT'ALBA
D) DOMINO'S

2

DO YOU KNOW WHICH ANIMAL CAN LIVE WITHOUT EATING FOR MORE THAN A YEAR?

A) BEAR
B) CAMEL
C) GREENLAND SHARK
D) CROCODILE

3

DO YOU KNOW WHAT IS THE HIGHEST CAPITAL CITY IN THE WORLD?

A) LA PAZ
B) KATHMANDU
C) MEXICO CITY
D) ADDIS ABABA

DO YOU KNOW WHICH IS THE ONLY INTEGER THAT HAS NO ROMAN NUMERAL EQUIVALENT?

A) ZERO
B) THOUSAND
C) FIVE
D) FOUR

DO YOU KNOW WHICH IS THE OLDEST LANGUAGE STILL SPOKEN TODAY?

A) GREEK
B) HEBREW
C) CHINESE
D) TAMIL

DO YOU KNOW WHICH COUNTRY HAS NEVER WON A GOLD MEDAL AT THE OLYMPICS?

A) INDIA
B) SWITZERLAND
C) BANGLADESH
D) EGYPT

DO YOU KNOW WHICH IS THE TALLEST STATUE IN THE WORLD?

A) STATUE OF LIBERTY
B) CHRIST THE REDEEMER
C) STATUE OF UNITY
D) GREAT BUDDHA OF LESHAN

DO YOU KNOW IN WHICH CITY THE FIRST TRAFFIC LIGHT WAS INSTALLED?

A) LONDON
B) NEW YORK
C) PARIS
D) BERLIN

DO YOU KNOW WHO INVENTED THE BALLPOINT PEN?

A) THOMAS EDISON
B) LÁSZLÓ BÍRÓ
C) NIKOLA TESLA
D) LEONARDO DA VINCI

DO YOU KNOW WHICH IS THE RAREST METAL ON EARTH?

A) GOLD
B) PLATINUM
C) RHODIUM
D) PALLADIUM

DO YOU KNOW WHICH IS THE LARGEST ORGAN IN THE HUMAN BODY?

A) LIVER
B) HEART
C) BRAIN
D) SKIN

DO YOU KNOW WHICH IS THE ONLY MAMMAL THAT CANNOT JUMP?

A) ELEPHANT
B) RHINOCEROS
C) BEAR
D) GIRAFFE

13

DO YOU KNOW WHICH COUNTRY HAS THE MOST TIME ZONES?

A) UNITED STATES
B) RUSSIA
C) CHINA
D) FRANCE

14

DO YOU KNOW WHICH IS THE ONLY FOOD THAT NEVER SPOILS?

A) SALT
B) HONEY
C) SUGAR
D) VINEGAR

15

DO YOU KNOW WHAT WAS THE FIRST PROGRAMMABLE COMPUTER?

A) ENIAC
B) ZUSE Z3
C) COLOSSUS
D) IBM 701

PARADOXES

DO YOU KNOW WHAT THE LIAR PARADOX IS?

THE LIAR PARADOX OCCURS WHEN A SENTENCE LIKE "I AM LYING" IS SPOKEN. IF THE STATEMENT IS TRUE, THEN IT IS FALSE, BUT IF IT IS FALSE, IT IS TRUE, CREATING A CONTRADICTION.

DO YOU KNOW WHAT ACHILLES AND THE TORTOISE PARADOX IS?

ACCORDING TO THIS PARADOX, ACHILLES CAN NEVER OVERTAKE THE TORTOISE IN A RACE BECAUSE EVERY TIME HE REACHES THE POINT WHERE THE TORTOISE WAS, THE TORTOISE HAS MOVED SLIGHTLY AHEAD. THIS PARADOX CHALLENGES THE CONCEPT OF CONTINUOUS MOVEMENT.

DO YOU KNOW WHAT RUSSELL'S PARADOX IS?

RUSSELL'S PARADOX INVOLVES THE SET OF ALL SETS THAT DO NOT CONTAIN THEMSELVES. IF A SET CONTAINS ITSELF, IT SHOULDN'T; BUT IF IT DOESN'T CONTAIN ITSELF, IT SHOULD. IT IS ONE OF THE FOUNDATIONAL ISSUES IN MODERN LOGIC.

DO YOU KNOW WHAT THE BIRTHDAY PARADOX IS?

THE BIRTHDAY PARADOX SHOWS THAT IN A GROUP OF 23 PEOPLE, THERE IS ABOUT A 50% CHANCE THAT TWO PEOPLE WILL SHARE THE SAME BIRTHDAY. THIS SURPRISING RESULT IS A CURIOSITY OF PROBABILITY.

DO YOU KNOW WHAT THE GRANDFATHER PARADOX IS?

THE GRANDFATHER PARADOX OCCURS WHEN, IN A TIME TRAVEL SCENARIO, SOMEONE GOES BACK IN TIME AND KILLS THEIR GRANDFATHER BEFORE HE HAS CHILDREN. IF THE GRANDFATHER DIES, THE TIME TRAVELER CANNOT BE BORN, BUT IF THEY AREN'T BORN, THEY CAN'T GO BACK IN TIME AND KILL THEIR GRANDFATHER, CREATING A CONTRADICTION.

DO YOU KNOW WHAT THE PARADOX OF THE EXISTENCE OF NOTHING IS?

THE PARADOX OF THE EXISTENCE OF NOTHING REFLECTS A LOGICAL CONTRADICTION: IF NOTHING EXISTS, THEN IT IS NO LONGER NOTHING, BECAUSE "TO EXIST" IMPLIES SOME FORM OF BEING. HOWEVER, IF NOTHING DOES NOT EXIST, THEN THE CONCEPT OF "NOTHING" ITSELF HAS NO MEANING. THIS PARADOX CHALLENGES THE CONCEPT OF EMPTINESS AND ABSENCE.

SOLUTIONS

1- c) Antica Pizzeria Port'Alba. Antica Pizzeria Port'Alba opened in Naples in 1738 and is considered the first pizzeria in the world.

2- d) Crocodile. Crocodiles can fast for extended periods, even over a year, by slowing their metabolism during periods of inactivity.

3- a) La Paz. La Paz, the administrative capital of Bolivia, is situated at around 3,640 meters (11,942 feet) above sea level, making it the highest capital city in the world.

4- a) Zero. The Romans had no symbol for zero, as their numbering system did not include it. The concept of zero was developed later in other cultures.

5- d) Tamil. Tamil is one of the oldest languages still in use today, dating back over 2,000 years. It is spoken primarily in southern India and Sri Lanka.

6- c) Bangladesh. Despite its population of over 160 million people, Bangladesh has never won a gold medal at the Olympics.

7- c) Statue of Unity. The Statue of Unity in India, depicting Sardar Vallabhbhai Patel, is the tallest statue in the world, standing at 182 meters (597 feet) tall.

8- a) London. The first traffic light was installed near the Palace of Westminster in London in 1868. It was designed to manage horse-drawn carriage traffic.

9- b) László Bíró. László Bíró, a Hungarian journalist, invented the ballpoint pen in 1938. In many countries, ballpoint pens are still called "biros" in his honor.

10- c) Rhodium. Rhodium is the rarest and one of the most valuable metals on Earth. It is primarily used in automobile catalytic converters.

11- d) Skin. The skin is the largest organ in the human body, with a surface area of about 2 square meters. It is essential for protection and temperature regulation.

12- a) Elephant. Elephants are the only mammals that cannot jump due to the structure of their legs and their enormous weight.

13- d) France. Surprisingly, France has the most time zones—12 in total—due to its numerous overseas territories scattered around the globe.

14- b) Honey. Honey is the only natural food that never spoils if stored properly. It has been found in ancient Egyptian tombs, thousands of years old, still edible.

15- b) Zuse Z3. The Zuse Z3, designed by Konrad Zuse in 1941, was the first functional programmable computer. It is considered a pivotal step in modern computing.